Contents

Your Life and Energy

You got up this morning. Perhaps an alarm clock went off or you switched on the radio. You may have switched on the light. If you live in a cold climate your bedroom was probably warm because you have heating.

What did you do next? Did you go to bathroom, have a wash in hot water? Did you then have some breakfast? Were you listening to the radio or watching television?

By then it must have been time to go to school. Did someone take you in a car or did you go by train or bus? When you arrived at school the heating may have been on for several hours, and the lights burning in your classroom. Lessons started. Was it your turn to work on the computer?

All these things we do nearly every day. We do not think about it much, but everything we do uses energy. Everything we eat or use has needed energy in order to make it. It took energy to light your home and get you to school. It took energy to heat your water, bake your bread, make your clothes. We use an enormous amount of energy.

▲ Machines that use energy are needed for many household tasks.

▶ Computers at home, and in schools, factories and offices, also use energy.